Know Your Worth: You Are Not Your Past

Know Your Worth: You Are Not Your Past

ROMONA JACKSON

WWW.13THANDJOAN.COM

WWW.13THANDJOAN.COM

Know Your Worth: You Are Not Your Past. Copyright 2019 by Romona Jackson. All rights reserved. No part of this publication may be reproduced, distributed, or transmitted in any form or by any means, including photocopying, recording, or other electronic or mechanical methods, without the prior written permission of the publisher, except in the case of brief quotations embodied in critical reviews and certain other noncommercial uses permitted by copyright law. For permission requests, write to the publisher, addressed "Attention: Permissions Coordinator," 500 N. Michigan Avenue, Suite #600, Chicago, IL 60611.

13th & Joan books may be purchased for educational, business or sales promotional use. For information, please email the Sales Department at sales@13thandjoan.com.

First Edition Printed, January 2019
Library of Congress Cataloging-in-Publication Data has been applied for.

ISBN: 978-1-7335154-5-0

Dedication

Thank you, God, for the experiences that led to this book and the story you are writing that I get to call my life! Thank you for every chapter because with each ending there is an amazingly beautiful beginning that only you can give!

I dedicate this book to my awesome mother who is the rock and foundation of my life! She taught me and continues to teach me how to be a lady! She teaches me resilience and strength, graced with love unconditionally! My mother is my angel wrapped in flesh that I get to embrace and with whom I can share my life. My mother is my loudest cheerleader and my toughest critic, but one whose love for me can never be questioned. She is my true source of inspiration in every way! If you want to know me, know her! If I can be half the woman that she is in my lifetime, I will be beyond successful!

Foreword

Reading a book where the author shares the depths of their soul on each page and the reader can almost hear their heartbeat with every word is a rare and exceptional find. The best of us have had experiences that we've found difficult to articulate for fear of being shamed; appearing strange or even extreme. When we finally read, hear or see exactly what we've been thinking, it seems an incredible bolt of lightning shoots through our bodies and our joy EXPLODES as our thoughts are validated and confirmed by someone else. Romona Jackson's Know Your Worth: You Are Not Your Past is the accelerant for which you've been waiting.

Reading her words took me back to our days as college roommates at Florida A&M University. Living in close quarters during the period she shares in the book; could never have prepared me to read her story detailed within these pages. I now have a better perspective on the experiences that we shared and the road each of us took in life. It's incredible that we've come full circle while realizing our worth as women and believers.

This book invites you into a deep and painful time in the author's life that she uses to draw upon for life-lessons that will bring value to every reader. Jackson eloquently, but more importantly unashamedly, shares how self-worth is defined and given value at an early stage in life through circumstances most would never consider. It will make every reader recount the steps of their lives in an attempt to find the initial place where value and worth were first imposed. In Know Your Worth: You Are Not Your Past, you will:

- Begin to identify where and how self-worth is assessed.
- Recognize effect and impact of negative self-image.
- Understand the correlation between a silent voice and personal power, poor, and acceptance.
- Identify subtle steps used to kill dreams and the overwhelming love God uses to resuscitate them.
- See your past as a platform for your future and not a press release for your shame.
- Unveil the power of truth and real love.

I have heard many people, through tears, desperation and heartbreak, share life stories of trauma and devastation that they believed changed the course of their lives and ended in brokenness, which led them to my office for spiritual guidance and counseling. Of the many things I've discovered, not only have these experiences shaped their lives and personalities, but they have also severely damaged their self-worth. When King David inquired of Mephibosheth in 2 Sam 9:7-8, Mephibosheth's response to the King's kindness was a reflection of his low self-worth, "What is your servant, that you should notice a dead dog like me?" Mephibosheth's physical disability, from being dropped and damaged, caused him to view himself as nothing more than a mangy dog. In 2 Samuel 19, Mephibosheth allowed his appearance to deteriorate to what he thought of himself, unkempt feet, untrimmed mustache, and unwashed clothes.

KNOWING or coming into the understanding of who you are, requires a willingness to ACCEPT the truth of YOU, which is often the antithesis of what your experiences communicate. The truth of your story and your experiences may not be pretty, but it is useful for loving you and gaining self-worth. Arriving at a place of readiness to believe something that seems unreal and impossible requires DENYING the false story that encapsulates you at the point of trauma and being brave enough to trust something that only becomes reality by an affirmative response through faith.

Like Mary, the mother of Jesus, getting past a thought process that inquires "HOW CAN THIS BE," and getting to "LET IT BE AS YOU HAVE SAID," is pivotal to accepting that You Are Not Your Past. I would rather trust what God says about me than stay in a place called Lo Debar, where Mephibosheth was.

Lo Debar allows you to stay in a place where no one will ever say more about you than you say about yourself. In this book, Romona Jackson eloquently proclaims, "You are what you accept.....what you accept will either decrease your value or increase it..... you teach people how to treat you by the way you treat yourself. If you do not know the value you bring, you will always allow yourself to be mistreated!"

The powerful words of freedom shared in this book will transform thinking concerning forever! I rejoice with exceeding great joy at recommending this book to anyone who has ever struggled with recognizing and accepting their worth. Every life experience has increased the value of your worth. I commend this book and recommend it to the world as we navigate every #METOO story.

Soli Deo Gloria!
Reverend Cynthia McCants
Senior Pastor of The New Gethsemane Baptist Church,
Middle Island, New York

Preface: Healing by Transparency

"Don't Look at the Chapter, Read the Entire Work!"

So many people look at the chapter of my life that they walked in on and draw the conclusion that everything was always peaches and cream, or butterflies and unicorns. Once I begin to share my story, they stand in amazement, and they all make the same comment and ask the same question: "I would have never guessed you've been through all of that! Can you please tell me how you did it and can you help me to do the same?" The aftermath of those discussions is this book! So many fail to reach the destiny that is set before them; not because God changed, but because of refusal to accept and believe what God has spoken. When we fail to receive the narrative that God has orchestrated over our lives, we fall victim to the fallacious rhetoric of the enemy! In this space, we cannot heal! We cannot let go of the mistakes or bad decisions that we made in our past, and we allow the enemy to keep us bound. I pray that as you read the words that are on each page of this book, they become the keys that you need to release the weight of what is keeping you tied to your past. I pray that these words catapult you on to a path that changes your mindset and allows you to know and embrace your worth, declaring that you are not your past!

Introduction: What I Thought Would Hurt Me, Ushered Me!

"There is so much purpose in what you have gone through! It was not in vain!"

The primary purpose of an usher, in any capacity, is to usher you from the back to the front! We walk in, and they walk in front, with hopes that you will follow. Often, we take a seat in the back, and the usher turns around and looks like...okay, but the view is so much better up here. Why do we take a back seat? Some say it is easier to leave, or avoid the crowds altogether, and others resolve to do what is most comfortable. When we go through things in life and take a vivid look at our past, we deem ourselves unworthy to receive a seat up front. Walking up to the front requires confidence and a sense of belonging and ownership of the concept that no matter what you belong there!

In this book, I share intimate moments of my life, not for sympathy or judgment but as a testament of what God can do with a person that feels unworthy. I want to reveal that we are so priceless and so valuable and once we walk into that realization and emerge from the cocoon that often holds us back, life will be amazing. In this book, we will candidly talk about the past and how to use it to catapult us into our future! We will learn of our worth and acceptance and how knowing these things will position us to fully receive all that God has and not abort our divine destiny because of how we view ourselves!

Table of Contents

Dedication v
Foreword vii
Preface: Healing by Transparency xi
Introduction: What I Thought Would Hurt Me, Ushered Me! xiii
   I. Worth 1
   II. He Called Me Daughter 7
   III. Past 17
   IV. Your Life, Holistically, Depends on It 25
   V. Acceptance 29
   VI. The Love Exchange 33
   VII. The Beautiful Wake Up Call 39
Epilogue: The Journey Wasn't Just For Me! 43
Hello Beautiful, ... 45
Connect with Author Romona Jackson 47

I. Worth

[wərTH]

NOUN
the value equivalent to that of someone or something under consideration; the level at which someone or something deserves to be valued or rated.

    When it was placed heavy on my heart to write this book, it took a long time before I sat down and started to pen the words. My first book which was a book of devotionals came a little easier because I was on a journey and I was writing daily, so I had managed to gather a collection. This time, it is different because I am speaking from an after stage in my life. After, I have gone through, after the experiences that have brought me to this point…I am speaking from my after, so I believe that is what makes this so different. I began to ask God to guide my hands because for me this book is special to my heart. I asked God to help me to search deep within and allow me to pull up everything that lied within the cracks and crevices of my soul. I want everyone who decides to read this book to feel it, to be able to relate to it and at some point, to see themselves and ultimately, see their way out!

    Most authors when they write, think about chapters and catchy chapter titles, but for this book, I wanted to talk and allow the words to flow. There is no rhyme or reason, whatever He speaks, I write, and as He reveals, I reveal. I wanted this book to speak my truth and to explain why I am so passionate about people not allowing their past to dictate who they are and where they are going to go. I want people to use their past as a trajectory tool that catapults them into their destiny. It is a beautiful thing to embrace your history and use it for good when all the enemy wants to do is use it for evil, (Genesis 50:20) use it to keep you down, and use it to keep you in bondage. The enemy would rejoice if you never realize the essence of your very being and if you never lived according to the fullness of your potential. I want to be able to talk through the pages and if you feel it then feel free to talk back to me and together, we will discover our real value and declare that we are not our past.

It took so long for me to love who I am and sometimes when you do not know who you are you fall victim to things in the quest to find yourself. You look for things in so many different faces and places, and you begin to resemble those things without even realizing that the image in the mirror is distorted and skewed and is nothing like the image God created you to be. I think it started way back in elementary school for me. I always tried to make friends and fit in. I was the chubby little girl, with the chubby cheeks and short ponytails. I was shy, self-conscious and introverted. I was a smart child and loved to write. My imagination was out of this world. Often, I pictured myself as a famous dancer or a singer in a place that was so far away from my reality. As an only child, growing up in Brooklyn, I was coined as a "latch-key" kid. I was the one who came home and had to lock the door and not open it for anyone or any reason until my parents came back. I wasn't allowed to have anyone in the house when no adults were at home. I'll admit, I tested those waters a time or two and got caught. The price I paid was one that I did not want ever to repay again, so I was lonely. Television became my friend, and

3

I was into Bruce Lee movies, all the funny sitcoms that were popular during those days. Shows like What's Happening, The Facts of Life (I loved Tootie! I even took out two of my teeth to look like her, go figure!), and Good Times. I knew every song that came on the radio and could sing them word for word. I did what any only child would do to be happy and to entertain themselves. Knowing what I was worth wasn't a thought in my mind, but unbeknownst to me, my worth was being formed.

I shared in my devotional that I was molested as a child for three years, locked away in a closet so I wouldn't tell ...my worth was being formed. As I stood in the dark closet, holding a Barbie doll, I will never forget, playing with her hair, I found myself asking questions like, "Why me?" "What did I do?" I don't remember crying. I remember waiting until the key turned in the front door and right before it opened, I was rushed out so that no one would know. I was forced to act as though everything was normal. My value and my worth was being calculated. I obviously meant nothing to the person who inflicted this hideous act on me, and no one else knew so I guess I chalked it up as the start of being worthless. Knowing your value starts at a young age. I would even go as far to say that it begins when you are in the womb. How you are carried and cared for throughout the pregnancy and ultimately when you come forth, and they give you a name, a name that you will answer to for the rest of your life has meaning.

What have they called you? Better yet, to what do you answer? Did they love you enough to speak into your life and call forth what they wanted you to be? Did they call you beautiful? Did they call you smart? Did they affirm to you that you can do anything? To the contrary, did they say you were bad? Did they call you good for nothing? Were you told that you would never amount to anything? Believe me; I was called everything. Some names I remember vividly, as they were names that scarred. Many of those names I kept harbored until God showed me the reflection of who I was through His Eyes and then I began to wear those names as badges of strength.

Not knowing your worth and value takes your voice, rendering you powerless. It takes away the very thing that could be your lifeline. If you think you are worthless and have no value, then you accept the unspoken belief that your words do not matter and that no one will listen to you. You begin to accept the notion that no one cares as your truth. In this space, you have nothing to say, and if you did, you wonder to whom would you even talk to? You question how you would begin to speak? Moreover, you wonder if you can trust and sadly, who, if anyone, would believe you? With this mindset, you keep it all in until it takes root and grows with you, further tainting the you that you are purposed to become. I never shared my feelings with anyone. I kept it all in because there were always things going on or I felt as though no one would understand. It wasn't that my mother didn't love me or that she wasn't there for me, that was so very far from the truth. I just didn't know how to express my inner thoughts and feelings. I was like the caged bird who couldn't sing. I kept it in, locked away and that became the building blocks of how I saw myself and the ingredients for what I would later accept.

When you do not value yourself, you accept anything. Trust me! You will because you begin to think that any attention is better than no attention. Any notice that you receive when in this headspace, you resolve to eat it up like a fat kid with cake, and you become obese with poison that slowly kills the inner you. This gives truth to that old saying...in the graves lies many talents and gifts that the world will never know or get to experience.

I am writing this book, as I watch the waves. There are waves on a body of water where there is no end in sight, and as the waves crash, memories flood my mind and I smile amid the peace and tranquility. I remember when I used to cry at these thoughts. I was in bondage. Now when I shed a tear, it is a tear of freedom and how good it feels to be free. I am free enough to share my heart on these pages. Moreover, even though I am opening myself up to folks that I may never get to meet, I hope that I can help with what I share amid transparency.

When I was young, a lady in the church that I grew up in, in Brooklyn, New York, who happened to be a good friend of the family heard me. I will never forget! I was standing in the choir, and she asked me to sing and the next thing I knew, she was calling my parents, and she told them that I had a voice. She said, "Mona can sing Y'all." It is incredible how the gifts that God gives you are the exact gifts that you will need to carry you through! Now mind you, this was double fold. I didn't think I had a voice, because of my thoughts of worthlessness, but now here stands someone who declared that I did have a voice and, guess what? It was a voice that was pretty good, and one that people needed to hear. She gave me my voice physically and spiritually! She gave power to the powerless! I am going to let that sit right there, and by the end of the book, you will catch that! She started me on my musical journey, and I sang more and more in the choir. I was extremely nervous, and I had so much to learn, but I was on my way. My value was beginning to take a turn. During this time, not only was my voice being developed for singing but also prayer.

On Sunday mornings, the choir gathered in the fellowship hall, donned in gray robes with purple accents before ministering, to pray. I remember being down there with just a few choir members, and one of the older ladies asked me to pray. I was like

"Who me?" I didn't know the first thing about prayer, let alone prayer in public but I was obedient, besides there were only a few of us, so if I messed up it would be okay, I mean I was a kid! To this day, I cannot remember how I started or finished, but what I remember is that when I began to pray, the entire fellowship hall went from being empty to being filled from front to back. When I finished praying, tears were flowing, people stood in line to hug me, and all I heard was the lady telling my Bishop, "You need to hear this young girl pray." Little did I know then that God was forming my spiritual worth, which is by far more valuable than anything I could ever imagine.

II. He Called Me Daughter

"The name that you are called brings forth what lies within! Be careful what you answer to!"

I never received a lot of affirmation when I was a child, so that is why it is so hard to receive compliments. After receiving a compliment from a friend of mine, I responded negatively, and she taught me a real-life lesson. She said, "Just say thank you. Now, let's try it again." She complimented me once more, and I said, "Thank you." She went on to inquire, "Now was that so hard? How did that feel?" "It felt pretty good," I responded. She said, "Mission accomplished! Never take away the blessing that people want to give you by being negative. If you didn't deserve it, they wouldn't give it, so accept gracefully." For me, that lesson was gracefully learned.

I looked up to my Bishop when I was young, he was the first Pastor I had, and he was a powerful one. I mean when he spoke, he commanded attention, and when he taught, you learned more than you ever thought you could. He was a master teacher in my book. He sat on the pulpit, regal and strong, as I recall moments in church, listening to him speak. One time as the choir gathered to the front to sing, he said, "I want to hear my daughter. Let my daughter sing." I didn't know whom Bishop was talking about because I didn't think he noticed me, but the choir director knew, and she handed me the mic. I was stunned. I sang "Teach Me, O Lord" and I heard him giving God praise and tears welled up in my eyes when I heard him say "Sing daughter!"

You are probably wondering why I am walking down memory lane with you so sporadically, so let me explain. You can never understand where a person stands if you do not know where they came from! You will never understand the praise until you understand the testimony! Your environment shapes who you are, how you think and what you value. Therefore, it is needful to recognize the pivotal points that helped to form a person's mindset and thought processes. The word *daughter* assigned value. It established a sense of belonging. Someone looked at me and looked beyond the ugliness and wanted me to be a part of their world. Now I thought that was awesome, but it gets even better! Not only did the Bishop call me daughter but God called me daughter and gave me the greatest gift ever!

John 1:12 (KJV) But as many as received him, to them gave He power to become the sons of God, even to them that believe on his name.

I was baptized December 11, 1983, at the age of fourteen years old. I will never forget it. I watched this movie that took the world by storm literally, called *The Day After*. That movie spoke about those who survived after the biggest catastrophe of the world had taken place. I came to church, and Bishop used that movie as the context of his sermon, *The Day After*. In this instance, he was talking about the day after the coming of Christ. He asked of us, "Will you be left behind when He comes? Will you go back with Him?" After that sermon, when the doors of the church were

opened for the acceptance of the invitation, I took that walk and started life with Christ. I sang in the choir and ushered on the usher board. I was sold out for Christ! I wanted more, I wanted whatever *It* was that caused the people in my church to dance, shout, cry, and run like somebody was chasing them; I wanted that! I wanted *It* bad! I began to pray, and I came to church looking for *It* to happen! I was wondering how I would know when I have *It*? How would *It* feel? I wondered if I would start dancing, or if I would hear something and take off running? I didn't know, but I waited with great anticipation. It seemed that the more I prayed, the more I waited with expectation.

Then, one morning as I marched in with the choir, we were singing a song and the words "He gave it to me. He gave *It* to me! Salvation, He gave it to me!" I felt my feet getting lighter, and I started to cry. The more I sang, the harder I cried! The more I thought about the words that I was singing, the lighter my feet got! The next thing I knew, there were two people at my side holding up both of my arms and all I heard was "Praise Him Baby! Praise Him!" It was the best feeling that I ever had, and I didn't want it to stop. Wow! I still get chills just thinking about it! I would have done anything to stay in that space forever. Not only did the Bishop want me but so did God! My relationship with God carried me through a lot during those times. I learned that He would always be with me and that He would never leave me. I never knew how this confirmation would play such a huge role in my life as I got older.

Fast forward a few years to when, I was preparing to start college at St John's University, in Jamaica, New York. I had lost weight and was becoming a lady. I didn't know it at the time, but I would eventually be exposed to a whole new world of people and freedoms that I had not known before. I was being introduced to young men and activities that I would not usually have known about but would soon experience. I am proud to say that I never drank, smoke or did drugs. Surprisingly enough, and maybe because it was all around, but I did like the boys! Oh, how I liked the boys! This is DANGEROUS if you do not know who you are, what you are and even more dangerous if you did not have anyone to guide you through the right and wrong ways to deal with the opposite sex.

Don't get me wrong I did not have a torrid past, but I had some experiences that I wish I could have skipped. When I look back over my life, I am glad that I went through it, because it shaped me and positioned me to teach others, such that they will not have to walk the same road I did. Guys wanted me because of my body and that one dimple that graced my smile. I laugh at that to this day. The men came in all sizes and shapes and I ate it up! When I went away to college, it was worse. I mean they were bolder and much more persuasive, and I was out of the arc of protection from my family, so there were no boundaries. Again, I didn't have a torrid past, but I experienced so many heartbreaks and disappointments that I can't even number. I did not know who honestly liked me, or who genuinely cared, and it was awful. I accepted what I should not have accepted because I didn't realize how valuable I was. People preyed on those who did not know their worth! They lurked on every corner.

Married men, single men, men of the cloth, oh my goodness, you name it, they approached me. It was to the point that I couldn't have a decent conversation with someone without them alluding to wanting more. I remember working at a radio station during college and the station owner was showing me the ropes when it came to sales. He said, "Tomorrow come to work with a shorter skirt and flash that dimple, and you will make all the sales you need without saying a word." I was mortified that my intelligence was insulted with tactless and sexist antics.

I remember every time I walked into the station, how he played a song with lyrics that said, "Black coffee, no sugar, no cream." The song was talking about a man's love for dark-skinned women. Now mind you, I love my complexion. I love the hue and the fact that makeup is not necessary, but I felt violated. Another instance a Pastor came in and told me all I had to do was say the word, and his checkbook was mine. Again, I was mortified! Why am I sharing this?

There is nothing new under the sun and the same tricks the enemy used to defeat you and cheat you of your worth, are still being used. You must know who you are and what you have to offer to not fall victim of this plight! Some may read this and think to themselves, *I do not have to worry about that, I never had to worry. I always knew who I was and who I am!* You are blessed! Unfortunately, we have more young women now who have no clue as to who they are, and they are wearing it as a cloak of pride. The young women that I speak of are everywhere we turn. They are half dressed, leaving nothing to the imagination. They are answering to every name, except their own. They are dancing to songs that degrade them beyond measure. They are putting down the books and picking up the gold digger's handbook, using language that makes grown men blush and entirely giving up their birthright and destiny! So, if you have never experienced this, we have a duty to help those who are suffering from it and to be an example! We must teach them boldly and proudly, without compromise what their worth is. We must find ways to instill in them that they are more valuable to this world than what they are giving themselves credit for being! If I can get behind them and pull down that skirt, pull up that blouse to hide that cleavage, and to teach them how to carry themselves in a manner that is conducive to a lady, it would be spectacular. I cringe at some of the things I hear being said and shown on social media. If they only knew! If they just knew how precious, they are! If they only knew what they were carrying! It is imperative that they recognize that they are rare jewels, cut from the Creator's original cloth! These girls that I speak of are His unique and masterful creation! Oh, how they would love themselves so much, if they understood who and WHOSE they are!

I do remember, oh so well, how that feels. It is a lonely place because you are never happy with whom God made you be and wishing you were someone different. Once God shows you who you are, you discover the true essence of beauty and the fact that it doesn't lie in the outer appearance. You are empowered in knowing that it radiates from the inside out. There is power in knowing that your worth is not predicated on the body but what the body houses. This is what causes that inner beauty. Your beauty lies in what makes you a beautiful soul. It was no mistake that God told us in His word that it is not what goes into man that defiles him but what comes out.

Have you ever looked at a person who looked gorgeous or someone who had that all-eyes-on-them appeal? They glide over to where you are like a dream so that you can get a closer view of all the goodness they possess, then they mess around and open their mouth and what was once pleasing to the eye becomes something straight out of a horror story! Everything that makes you who you are lies within. No amount of makeup, designer dresses, Apple Bottom Jeans, or boots with the fur, can make you beautiful. If we are ugly on the inside, we are ugly on the outside. Beauty is an inside job!

Worth

You are so valuable! Every ounce of your being is worth far more than any treasure on this earth. God took time to speak you into existence. He took him time to create you, mold you, and to breathe His precious breath of life into you so that you can be who you are today. No element of your past can change that. He knew who you were before and He still called you! He knew the mistakes that you would make, and He knew the paths that you would divert towards, yet He still loves you and holds you in the palm of His hands and calls you the apple of His eye. So, if the Creator of all creation can look upon you and forgive you and not hold your past against you or diminish your value because of the wrong turns in life that you may have taken or those that you may still choose, why should you?

I believe, wholeheartedly, by virtue of my experience alone, that this is one of the biggest tricks of the enemy. If he can keep us replaying the same tape of our mistakes over and over in our minds, he will always keep us in a vicious cycle, that will continue to feed into his plan to abort our destiny! He is cunning and stealth with his wiles so much so that he gets you caught up in his web, leaving you wondering how you got here in the first place? That is the beginning of so many morning-after stories. Smooth talking guy, steps in and flashes a smile and the next thing you know, you are trying to undo what can't be undone, while he is on to the next one. Life is about being real and having real talk with ourselves. Too many times people sugar coat things that should not be sugar coated because we are people of the cloth but when we look at Jesus' ministry, we can learn that Jesus never sugar coated anything. He called it like it was, how it was and if it stepped on your toes, oh well, say "ouch", get right and keep on moving. That is not the place where we are right now. People are afraid to tell their truth because of what people may think or say and because of this many young girls and boys are losing their value by the *life full* (forget handful), because no one will stop and tell them the real hard truth. We need to empower youth so that they can think twice about making decisions. We are living in a time and space where children are killing themselves because they are bullied, and trying to alter themselves because of what they see on social media that is being glamorized. They are losing their innocence at an age that was unthinkable at one point in time. Babies are having more babies, while the mothers are concerned with being called grandma. This is not a judgment but more of a clarion call to WAKE UP, STAY WOKE and to start learning your value and your worth. When we honor our worth, we can pass it down to the next generation and watch future generations, (the ones we are blessed to see), break curses, become trendsetters of good and become productive men and women that impact the world with their presence!

    I went through a host of things in my life to bring me to this point and for this book. I know what it is like to not know your worth and ultimately, get to a place where you thought the world would be better off without you being in it. I have experienced these feelings not once, not twice, but many times. I stated earlier that I wanted to talk and here we are! I am not ashamed of what I experienced because it made me ROMONA. The good, bad and the ugly is all a part of my story. It all has purpose! You do not feel that way when you are going through but when God allows you to see the purpose for your pain, it is then that you understand, and you can declare that when you know your worth, that knowledge is unshakeable, empowering and most importantly, it requires validation from no one!

    I used to think I wasn't good enough, and I was always questioning who I am. When relationships didn't work, I blamed myself. When I fell into debt and couldn't get credit to save my life, I beat myself up daily. I wore my divorce like a scarlet letter and sank deeper and deeper into a bottomless abyss while those who claimed they were my friends and those claiming to be praying for me were doing just the opposite. Be careful about those quick to run to your aid during your downfall and slow to offer praise during your uprising. These people reveal their place in your life, and if you hang on to them, you are blocking the way for those who God truly wants to place around you to be a blessing and those whom you can bless. I can count my friends on maybe two hands, and I am so happy because my life is drama free. I don't know nothing and don't want to know nothing. I am okay going home and being with MONA because I love me enough to protect myself from things that will bring me back to that place of darkness and unfulfillment! Don't bring me a bone and I will not give you one to carry! Bad grammar but true-life wisdom!

God put me in a place of isolation and to some extent, even as I write this book, I believe I am still in that place. Today, I like to call it a *holding pattern* and day by day, He is giving me the signal from the tower that it is almost time for take off! You cannot know your value or your worth in the midst of a crowd. You feel me? How can God, in His eloquent whisper, speak *life* to you when you are surrounded with chatter? Chatter has no meaning, and drowns out the *life* giver. God wants to teach you what you are worth and what you mean to Him. He wants to reveal to what He was thinking about when He had you on the Potter's Wheel, spinning around and around, molding you and making you with His Masterful Hands! God wants you to witness His shaping of you and His efforts to define your every curve. He wants to share with you why you were kissed by melanin the way that you are, why your nose is shaped that way, and why you are voluptuous and not thin. He desires you to honor the way in which He anointed you! He wants to share with you why that relationship didn't work, or why he or she had to leave! He wants you to witness, in full transparency, why you had to go through that pain, and why you had to lie on your sick bed for a moment. When He reveals all, you will realize that the answer to each query is one that has a cost associated with it. Each of these factors lends to your value and makes you even more precious and priceless to those that behold you! You will learn that your worth was so miraculous that the Creator, left His throne to pay the ultimate price for you!

Once you know why, you can walk proudly, and boldly and not hold your head down in shame because of your past! You will be empowered to stand tall and confidently with a smile that won't quit because you know what you are worth! My spirit is leaping all over the place as God gives me these words to share with you! I cannot type fast enough! I hope you get what I am saying, and that you let it rest and marinate in your spirit. He loves us just that much! He doesn't want us wondering, thinking of ways to extinguish the fire of life He has placed within us. He doesn't want us considering cutting off our very existence, thereby taking with us the key that He gave to us to unlock another person's hope and destiny because they see that we made it through what they are going through. He wants us to be a light that shines as a witness to the fact that we were not destroyed, which in turn gives them hope that God will deliver them also!

III. Past

[past, pahst]

of, having existed in, or having occurred during a time previous to the present; bygone:

You Are Not What You Past Says You Are!

If the past had its way, it would rob you of your future. We must also remember that perspective is everything. If your past is not viewed in a healthy way, it can prove to be detrimental to life not yet lived. You can look at your past as a tool of progression or as a shackle. Being shackled by every negative experience that you have gone through is the ultimate bondage. You will find your feet and ankles shackled, your hands shackled, and your neck shackled, rendering you immobile. However, repeat after me, "YOU ARE NOT YOUR PAST!" I do not care what you have done, or where you have been, your past does not determine your future! It doesn't matter what Big Momma said to you! It doesn't matter who doubts your sincerity when you take that step towards the altar when God pricks your heart during altar call! No matter how many times you may have messed up doing the same thing that you vowed that you would not when you truly repent, God is there with outstretched arms. What others think or feel should not matter.

I was so fixed on what people thought of me that it consumed me. I didn't want to do any wrong and wanted to please people.

In my plight, I did the opposite and ended up hurting myself. When you hurt yourself for the sake of others, that is a dangerous place to be. You find yourself caring for everybody except you, and giving up on your dreams, while others live theirs and then you find yourself living with regret.

Contrary to what others believe, there is a balance. We have to be open and ready to receive it when it presents itself. You can love and support and still be you and do what makes you happy, but it takes the wisdom and the guidance of God to teach you how to do this successfully.

When I embraced the fact that sometimes we go through obstacles, not just for the sake of ourselves but for others, I began to operate differently. Operating from a place of empowerment helped me to balance things. I knew that if I was in that person's life, it was for more than just the initial purpose, but there was maybe something I needed to share or help to bring out or to help them to move past. I believe that everyone needs someone in their life that will help them to see beyond what they have gone through and to see the beauty in it all. I desired to be that person for whomever God gave me. He gave me another sight, and this may sound weird, but I was able to see what they were not showing me and that is what I also need to address. On that note, let me pause and give you a disclaimer. You must be careful with whom you share with, because everyone may not be able to handle your truth! Taking a line from that famous movie where the character yelled, "YOU CAN'T HANDLE THE TRUTH!" Oh, how true this statement is. If you reveal before God's appointed time, it can become a stumbling block! That is why we must tune in and listen to God to give us the okay to share. At that point, our sharing becomes a tool of transformation!

When you break free from the presumed condemnation of your past, it will allow you to step into the places that God has called you to go. It will cause you to walk through doors that were always open for you, but because your view was clouded by your past, you saw the open door as closed. God is so gracious, such that He will keep the door of opportunity open so you can walk through it! I remember when I took the first sip of loving myself. It was so freeing. I also struggled to find the balance at the same time because I had always allowed thoughts to creep in that would make me take two steps backward. I had to continually remind myself that my past did not define my future. Yes, my past had played a role in shaping me, but it didn't represent my final destination! God had so much more for me to do, and so many places for me to go. I had faith enough to believe that I was going to get there, so I shut down the voice of my past and pressed forward.

I love butterflies. Sure this is an odd segway, but I do. And I will share why. It seemed that at every stage of my life that I just needed a reminder that God was near, a butterfly appeared. There were times that may not have been viewed as a happy stage in my life, and moments when decisions needed to be made and I was in search of answers. It amazed me that a butterfly would appear. I also love them because they embody the essence of transformation. To take something that was once viewed as ugly (your past) aka the caterpillar and to watch it wrap itself up in a cocoon and go through a metamorphosis, which requires breaking, reshaping, growth and development over a period of time only to emerge as something so beautiful and graceful is just stunning. The beauty lies in the fact that it looked nothing like it was before. The butterfly allows the process of transformation to usher them into one of the most fascinating and admirable creatures that exist today. Taking note of this caused me to conclude, that if we allow our past to be our cocoon and we allow it to make us, to shape us, to form us and to take every aspect of what we went through, we too can bear witness to the beauty of the life that God wants for us. Instead of allowing our past to hamper us, we will emerge, just as the butterfly emerges, beautiful and admired because we gave God our ashes and in return, He gave us beauty. (Isaiah 61:1-3)

Embracing our past also empowers us. There are a few things that I have learned in my life, and one of the lessons is that what you do not face, cripples you. If we are afraid to face the things that we have gone through and to look it square in the eye, we will never learn from it, and it will always have the proverbial upper hand. We have to be able to look at the things that we wish to hide and uncover them. We must take control of our lives by removing all the cobwebs and blowing off the dust, standing up in power and strength to proclaim that it "No longer has dominion over us and we will be free from it." The word of God tells us so eloquently in

Psalm 103:10-12," He does not treat us as our sins deserve or repay us according to our iniquities. For as high as the heavens are above the earth, so great is His love for those who fear him; as far as the east is from the west, so far has He removed our transgressions from us." So why do we wear our past like a ball and chain when God does not? A considerable part of this is found wrapped up in the very act of forgiving ourselves.

When you do not forgive someone, it is easy for you to recall what they did to you. I mean, you remember the day, and the time, right down to the millisecond! You remember where you were, and what you were wearing, and you hold on to that memory in an unforgiving state. Moreover, every time there is an opportunity to move forward, you are there to pull it back with those famous words, "I will never forget what you did!" That is such a harsh thing to do to people. Never releasing others when God has so graciously released you is a harmful act! If you think it is hard on another person, imagine what it is like when it is self-inflicted. Imagine the damage being done when the one person that you cannot seem to forgive is the very one who is looking right back at you in the mirror. You beat yourself up by making statements like, "I thought I was smarter than that", "I cannot believe I fell for it again", "How could I have let myself get so deep into this", and "I should have known better". Does any of this sound familiar? It's those words that you speak that ties the ropes of bondage around your body tighter and tighter until you are marked and bruised with new scars and new pains and new disappointments because you keep reliving what you should have let go.

Then the enemy knows when he has you right where he wants you! He is all up in your headspace, so then he takes it a step further and those negative mantras that kept replaying over and over now become…"Nobody will ever love me because of what I have done", "I don't deserve to be happy," "It will never happen for me," or "God can never use me!" The more you rehearse those things in your mind, the more you forget what the word of God says about you. You stunt your growth, and you stay right there, wallowing in a mess that you do not belong in, as your destiny awaits. Ask me how I know about this space and my response is that "I know because I lived there!" My favorite statement was "No one understands me!" Let me tell you when the enemy got all in my headspace, I found the right sad song, I turned off all the lights and cried until I couldn't breathe, and when it was over, I asked myself if all of it had solved anything? My answer was absolutely nothing! All I had to show for what I had taken myself through was red, puffy eyes, a stopped-up nose, and a dead cell phone battery because the song played over and over!

As I said a few times, this is real talk. We are just talking, and I want to be real! The only way I can encourage you to KNOW YOUR WORTH and help you to declare, with all the authority and power that God has bestowed upon you, that YOU ARE NOT YOUR PAST is to tell you where I was and then to show you how I overcame! It is not easy, but it is necessary. It is essential for you to grow. Regardless of what your past looked like, what is significant to you may not be substantial to another, but all of that doesn't matter because the hold it has on you is still the same. The power of the bondage that aims to stop you from reaching your rightful place in Him is still the same. Let me give you a simple analogy that God just released in my spirit about the past that you are holding. Let's consider a magnifying glass. What is the sole purpose of a magnifying glass? To make things more significant than what they appear so that you can see it better. When you take the magnifying glass away, it is not as big, and you find that you are bigger than what you were observing. This perspective or view can equate to power. Now, let's consider your past. The enemy wants to magnify it in your mind, so when you think about it, in an unhealthy manner, you make it bigger than what it is. This magnification is a distorted view of reality, and it causes your focus to change. It creates the thoughts that you have about yourself to change. However, once we remove the thing that is causing the past to be magnified, in other words, change our mindset about our past, we can see where we stand and where we are. Lastly, we must learn to accept the reality of where we are and honor the fact that our past can no longer hinder or overshadow the future that God has planned for us.

Stand in the truth of your past and allow it to cause your light to shine brighter. No matter what your reality is and what it contained, it was a part of making you who you are. It made you stronger and wiser and oh so much better! Without the detours in life, we would not be able to appreciate where we stand today. What we went through, we survived for a reason! Some people faced that same mountain that you had to climb and others had to go down deep into that same valley that you had to cross and didn't make it, but you did! I spoke about being divorced in my first book and some of the things I experienced as a result of the unpopular decision that I made. What people did not know was that months before even walking down the aisle, the Lord gave me so many signs that I chose to ignore. God did not sanction my marriage. He waved so many red flags in front of me that it should have been hard for me to miss them, but I wanted to be married. When God's PERMISSIVE will allowed it, He was silent through it all. This is the loneliest place ever to be.

Looking back, I am not sad. I do not have any regrets. I do not feel ashamed about the decision that was made. During that tumultuous time in my life, I met some people that thought they wouldn't survive, and some who didn't know if they could stand. I was the complete opposite. Allow me to be transparent, and please understand, no one gets married to get divorced, but this was the path that I traveled. While traveling, God revealed and moved people whom I thought were for me because they chose to believe and not verify! I found myself in it all. I began to learn about me and what makes me who I am. The most beautiful revelation that God has allowed me to witness in the seven years that I have been in this season was how to love. I will talk about love a little later in this book. It was in love that I learned to embrace this part of my past. I accepted and was not swayed by the crowd of folks who should have been concerned with the matters of their own lives. I wouldn't trade where I am right now in my life for anything in the world. I love my life, and I am so excited about the plans God has for me!

IV. Your Life, Holistically, Depends on It

"Love yourself enough that you will do what it takes to take care of you in every aspect of your being."

How you view yourself and what you have been through can positively or adversely affect how you treat yourself physically, spiritually, financially and emotionally. It's all connected. Your perception of self also manifests in your relationships. You attract who and what you are. You send signals that tell a person all about you, in some instances, from a first glance or at the moment you say "hello." They will either ignore you or stop, stare and say, "Wait you had me at hello!"

When you walk in the room, does the atmosphere shift or does it remain the same? Do you enter as if you belong or do you get smaller and lost in the crowd? The answer, again, lies in how you view yourself. I am not talking about vanity or anything that would cause you to think more of yourself than you should, but I am talking about the innate confidence that comes when you know who you are and whose you are. Power is that glow that shines because He radiates through you, that smile you wear because you have unspeakable joy and that glory that allows you to recognize that no matter what, your happiness cannot be altered. The world cannot take it from you because the world didn't give it to you. Happiness is that peace you have that holds you up because you know that your hope is built on nothing less than Jesus' blood and righteousness! I ask again what happens when you enter a room?

If you allow your past to diminish your worth, you will more than likely emanate that when you interact with others. You will not speak up, and you will not stand tall because your past has led you to believe that you are not worthy enough to stand where God has placed you. You will allow yourself to ask questions like "Why did they ask me? There are so many people who are better." I was notorious about this when it came to my singing. I love to sing and used to pray about it as a child, and I would ask God to give me a voice. I used to sing and sing. Now it was not always pleasant to the ear, but one day God changed that.

When asked to sing I would always find a reason not to because I was either shy or thought that my voice wasn't good enough. I thought my voice wasn't full enough or that I couldn't holler like some. I would convince myself that I could not do the vocal acrobats. I deemed myself unfit, so I did not fully operate in the abilities that God had given me. God forbid if someone had to sing before I did, and they were excellent, I prayed that a huge hole would open and swallow me up so that I could avoid the embarrassment. I remember being on program to sing and i had no idea that a recording artist was to sing before me, I panicked! When it was over she came up to me and hugged me and I told her that if I knew she was singing I would not have! She looked at me and said "don't ever deny the world of your gift! Use it no matter what!" I will remember those words forever!

My feelings about my voice all changed when I was in my home church in Brooklyn, and I was approached by someone who was visiting. They revealed to me that they were on the verge of suicide and came to church to hear something that would help bring comfort and when they heard me sing, it was the start of what they needed. I then realized that the gift I was given, should not be compared to the gift of another. I recognized that it was to be used to bring glory to the Father and to help draw people unto Him. Had I continued in that same vein of feeling unworthy, I would have missed my assignment. If you are placed in purpose, it is because God deemed you worthy! Let me remind you, God knows all about what you have done and what you will do in advance, yet He still calls us. He loved us enough to entrust us with His precious gift, and we must show our gratitude by caring for it and using it every time we are afforded the opportunity to do so!

Our worth is also shown by the way we take care of our bodies. When you know your worth, you will value the temple that God uses to carry the anointing He bestowed upon you. You will not treat it any less than you should. You will eat right, and you will exercise, you will not put it through unnecessary stress and strain day by day. You are valuable, and you should not ever let the past dictate how you look or feel. When you have been delivered, show some sign! When you have been set free, do not be afraid to carry yourself in such a way that leads people to ask, What causes you to act this way?" Showing the world that you have been set free will give you another way to tell your story and another form of sharing about how the Lord has delivered you. This will also provoke them to want to know a little bit more about your Jesus and to try Him and see if He can do for them what He has done for you!

V. Acceptance

"When accept that your past does not determine your future, you will walk in full freedom!"

    You are what you accept. What do I mean by that? Exactly what it says. What you accept will either decrease your value or increase it. You have always heard that you teach people how to treat you by the way you treat yourself. If you do not know the value that you bring to the table, then you will always allow yourself to be mistreated! You are a treasure! A rare jewel! You carry the anointing of God in your belly, and that makes you a big deal! You are an heir to royalty!

    To the average person, you are average. If you are not living what folks are now chanting, *your best life*, which only God knows what that entails, you are just ordinary. However, to God, you are not. You are above average. You are above mediocrity, because you were fashioned after His Image and that, my beautiful one, makes you more than extraordinary, so walk in it. What you accept is a critical point in knowing the value of who you are. I wrote earlier, that when you are not sure of your value and what you have to offer, you will accept anything. You will accept being mistreated because you have nothing from which to compare. That is why knowing the Word of God and allowing Him to teach you is paramount. Reading His Word about the love He has for you as His child will set the bar of what you should look for in your life. God loves us so much, and all He wants is for us to experience that love to the point that He went to great lengths to prove it.

One of the hardest things for me to do was to set the bar for what I would accept. I would always make excuses for why I allowed things such that now when I reflect, I recognize things I accepted from the past that I would never accept at this stage in my life. I didn't love me. Dare I say; I didn't respect myself. That sounds harsh, right? I know. How can a person not respect themselves? It is possible; trust and believe, it is. I thought that the ill-treatment was a byproduct of my wrongdoing, so I accepted it thereby causing disrespect to ensue. I looked at it as compensation for the wrongs of my past. I felt like I didn't deserve the flowers, hugs, kind words, admiration or the platforms. I had convinced myself that I didn't deserve for anyone to look at me and see more than what I saw within myself, I was so wrong.

God does not operate that way. I cannot say it enough; God does not see you where you are right now, He does not see you for your past. He calls forth the person that He knows you will be. He takes the broken, battered and tattered person that life spit out and left for ridicule, shame and death and shapes, them into a vessel that He can affectionately call Pastor, Evangelist, Missionary, Psalmist and the most beautiful names of all, My Child, My Friend! He allows us to represent Him and to be His Mouthpiece!

Therefore, you cannot just accept anything. Take off that cloak of shame, darkness, and unworthiness and put on the coat of many amazing colors that He made just for you. Walk in the Favor of God! Let His Favor, exude from your inner being, through your pores and saturate you with such loveliness that you do not have to explain to anyone how they should treat you. When you love yourself, they will already know and dare not treat you any differently.

 Be aware that deciding what you will accept will determine, in large part, the places you will go, conversations you will have, and the things that you will allow yourself to hear. This demeanor will cause you to wear a "No Dumping" sign and a "No Vacancy" sign when things try to enter your space that interferes with your value. You are too valuable to engage in things that will tarnish you. There will be no space in your mental and spiritual cache for gossip, back-biting, sowing discord, and overall negativity. Those things must flee. So, expect your circle of "friends" to shrink! Get ready for the labels that those people who cannot accept that you value yourself more than you value non-edifying shenanigans tend to place on you. This can be uncomfortable as the people around you shift. Be not dismayed. You know what? Here is an even better action...Welcome it! Embrace it! If shifting is happening, then it means your value is shining forth, and that is precisely where you want to be. This shift in the atmosphere will open the doors to so many excellent chapters in your life.

VI. The Love Exchange

"Sometimes God has to get you ready for your promise and your promise ready for you!"

Song of Solomon 6:3A: "I am my beloved's, and my beloved is mine."

As I bring all of my thoughts to a close, I am led to speak about love. This is a chapter that may seem different but one that most want to have included in the story of their lives. Love is our Creator! 1 John 4:8 and 16B declare God is Love! He is Love. I believe that desiring and wanting love is not a bad thing. Love is one of the greatest sentiments to desire because ultimately, you wish to have Him, more of Him. A love that can be shared by two different people, who decide to connect worlds and to create, with God at the center, is representative of all that He orchestrated love to be.

I firmly believe that to gain access to love in this capacity, all of the things that we have discussed up to this point, have to be in line. Before God releases us to experience love, he wants us to be whole. Mathematically, two halves do make a whole, but there is still a place of brokenness that can exist without God's repair. In this instance, we cannot be entirely made whole in His absence. He must be a part of the equation.

I have not found my true love or better, yet my true love has not found me, but I know he is on the way. While I wait, I ask God to prepare me to be the person that I need to be for this man. The Bible is clear in Proverbs 18:22, that when a man finds a wife, he findeth a good thing and obtains favor from the Lord. I have heard this scripture time and time again, and it was not until now that I truly understood its essence. Favor is present when we gain approval, acceptance or special blessings and benefits from God. I have even seen it defined as "demonstrated delight." Imagine God finding delight in the man who seeks Him for the partner he is to have in life. Can you imagine how that life would manifest? I do not insinuate that it would be a life free from the challenges of the world that often plagues us, but it will be one that can withstand those challenges because it is founded in Him. There is nothing that God will not see it through.

To be a help-meet is to be a partner in life, and someone with whom you can build, achieve and, discover common ground. I used to think that a relationship was all about love! There is so much more. The display of the moments when he pushes you, and you drive him, and the times when you strengthen him, and he reinforces you are what sustains love. The display of love is through action. Even if he loves me, and I love him, we must consider what happens when circumstances arise that calls that love into question? What happens when something transpires that shakes the very foundation of that love? What happens when the makeup comes off, and the extra pounds come on? What happens when sickness knocks at the door? Can love stand on its own and be enough? Is it really enough? I have found that it is not. You must have so much more. There must be so much more substance in a relationship for it to thrive. These sentiments, depict the prime reason why you cannot enter into a relationship without

knowing your value and your worth. You must be whole to sustain in a relationship with another person. If you enter into a relationship broken, it is already a set up for disaster. Unfortunately, I learned this lesson the hard way, but in retrospect, it is fortunate because now I know.

    I can remember times that I would sit, and watch those that were together, and I used to get all in my feelings. I know that is laughable, but while I am waiting, God is trying to teach me. He is teaching me to be patient and to not be in a rush. He is teaching me that my time is not His time and if I want what He has for me, love that will stand the test of time, I must be patient. What He has is far better than anything I could have ever conjured up in my thoughts and dreams. I want to be chosen by my mate, the same way that God chose me. God said that no matter what I did or what I have done, no one can change the fact that He has chosen me. His love for me is a choice. He could have chosen so many others, but He chose me! Despite what I looked like, despite the mistakes I made, He chose me, and because He chose me, I will wait until the one He has kept for me, finds and chooses me. They will love me and have the same acceptance of me that God has, which will be a love that is unmatched! That is my prayer! I am praying to experience love the way God intended. I want to know what it truly feels like to have someone look into my eyes and see Mona and love Mona and then I will have the distinct pleasure and privilege to do the same. I want to know what it feels like to be with someone who loves me the way that Christ loved the Church. That has to be an amazing love.

    To find a mate who loves like the love that God gives has to be just as dynamic as the day that I indeed began to love myself. Loving myself has taught me and continues to show me how to love someone else. Love is an actual exchange that is not always divided 50/50. There may be times where one is giving more than the other. It is not with ill intent, but it may be the season that's being faced at that moment. Sometimes it means an exchange of strength or a transfer of wisdom. Whatever it may be, it all amounts to a genuine dialogue of the desire to live separate but to merge as one.

Again, knowing who you are and what you have to offer makes it easier to focus on building a foundation that will last and not be one that is superficial. When you know who you are it shows and will be attractive to those who think like you and want the same things as you. You will not have to settle. When you know your worth, you will know who you are and what makes you happy. This will release your partner of the vast array of mind games they have to play because you want them to make you happy. How can they make you happy when you do not even know how to make you happy? That is a huge responsibility to place on someone and one that some are not willing to take on.

Take time to know you. Watch, observe and be ever prayerful. I have hope and confidence that my love story is not over, and that my chance to experience the love that God intended is not over. I believe that God is a God of second chances and that my time is coming. I believe that your time is coming if you are in your waiting season like me. Until then, don't let it consume your thoughts. Live wholeheartedly for Him. LOVE ON GOD and serve Him with your whole heart, mind, body and soul. Don't miss this opportunity for it to be just you and God. Take this time to feel the love He wishes to shower down upon you.

Embrace the late in the midnight hour hugs. Enjoy the way He wipes your tears and sings over you. Enjoy serving Him passionately. Enjoy how He fills every void and how He ushers you to the Throne of His Grace with every encounter. Bask in the way He shares His Heart and plans for your life. Enjoy it being just Him and you. Paul said in 1 Corinthians 7:7, "But I wish that everyone would be single, just as I am, yet every person has a special gift from God, of one kind or another." Paul knew that if we were single, our primary focus would be to serve God but Paul also knew that everyone did not possess the gift of singleness.

While you are waiting, serve Him, and before you know it, God will grant you the very petition of your heart. He will send you the one that is within His will and plan for your life! He will send you the one that will honor Him and bring glory to Him. Having a boo is easy! It is easy to have a babe! It is a blessing, and a gift to a have a partner in life who will speak to the areas of that no one else can. Love yourself with a love that only God can give. See the very places of your soul that makes you who you are. That is worth the wait.

VII. The Beautiful Wake Up Call

"No sound is more beautiful than the sound of you awakening to YOU!"

WAKE UP! This is your WAKE-UP call that says "You are beautiful!" We have talked about knowing our worth, allowing our past to shape and mold us. We have talked about taking care of ourselves and redefining what we will and will not accept. We have learned and continue to learn that we have so much worth, that our value, by virtue of whom God made us, makes us priceless. There will never be another like (insert your name right here)! We can declare that "When God made me, he broke the mold! I have my own unique DNA and my unique fingerprint! My voice is unique! My walk is unique! My personality is unique!" Allow me a moment to introduce to some and present to others the fact I am a unique and beautiful creation of God, and nothing can change that!

When I truly believed the power in declaring my worth, my life changed. When I changed how I viewed myself, my life gained a new purpose. I saw myself for whom God made me and I began to walk in it, and it is so liberating. I am comfortable in the skin I am in, and I wear my skin well! I am confident because I know what I bring to the table. I know that what I went through does not define me or determine my future. My history doesn't confine me within barriers and constraints that prohibit me from walking the path which God has called me. I accept every aspect of my life, and I welcome the new horizons I have yet to experience. Beautiful, you are, not your past! You are not the chains and shackles that attempt to present themselves to you as the end all and the be all. That is not whom God called you to be. If you find yourself in a place where you are stuck, a place where you cannot move forward because backward seems to be the only gear that is working, pray that God begins to open your eyes to who you are in Him. Ask Him to open your heart to receive the love He has for you, and in turn, you will begin to love whom He has made you be.

The key to all of this is that you have to want to be better. You must want to let go. You have to desire to live the abundant life that God promised you. I say this with all sincerity because some people love to be miserable. They enjoy wallowing in the pig trough because that is all they can see themselves accomplishing. They lose hope because they refuse to believe the report of the Lord and they choose to accept the negative rhetoric of the world that says that you cannot be more than what you are right now and that you cannot be more than the cards that life has dealt you.

There are others who choose to trade their value for popularity. Those that want to "level up" and be upgraded, according to the world's standards because it looks good until they find that what they have been patterning their life after is counterfeit and has nothing to offer but dead ends and disappointments. Do you know what the awesome thing about all of this is? It is never too late to recognize who you are and to begin to walk in it. The first step is to seek God! The second step is to surround yourself with like-minded people who can appreciate the roads you have traveled and the people who are ready to grab you by the hand and say "LET'S GO!"

You can only be your best in the presence of people who can see beyond the surface and those that begin to call forth that which you cannot see. You need people who can pray and people who can fast for you. You need people who are not afraid to tell you when you are wrong and those who can love you past the pain and the hurt. You will also require people who will hold you in the middle of all the chaos and intercede on your behalf until God answers, or until it rains down from Heaven.

Your purpose also calls for people who will rejoice with you and those who are not easily dimmed by your shine. Find those who can take out their proverbial cloth and shine you until they see their reflection in your glow because they know when their time comes, you will do the same and at times more for them. These people who possess the attributes that I speak of are your squad, your vision keepers, and dream pushers. Your squad knows your worth, and they value you. Your squad will also alert you not to engage in anything that will dim your light. Moreover, if anyone tries to tear you down maliciously, they will fight for you!

Know your worth! You are NOT your past! You are the essence of all God intended personified! Your life is a living epistle. People will read your story and know God! They will learn about your life and see that they can be victorious! You are a living testimony!

Epilogue: The Journey Wasn't Just For Me!

I thank everyone who thought it not robbery to read the words that were given to me to place between the pages of this book. My prayer is that through my transparency you can see that God has a purpose for everything. The promise that He made in His word that tells us that He will give you beauty for your ashes is true! I am absolutely, positively in LOVE with every aspect of who I am and the path my life is on! When you see me smile, it is genuine! When you see me sing and praise Him, you now know a piece of the story behind my praise and why I LOVE me some HIM! Everything that I was allowed to experience, (because you know God has to give permission), has made me into the Lady I am! Tell yourself that you have a PURPOSE! You are being formed, shaped and molded, so enjoy the journey! God's got you, and He knows exactly what it will take to get you there; NEVER putting more on you than you can bear. The Love He has for us is UNMATCHED, and He loves on us just like a doting Father. Accept His Love and begin to ask Him to allow you to see who you are through His Eyes. I promise, once you get a glimpse of His beautiful depiction of you, you will never accept anything less than what He has to give!

Hello Beautiful,

When I think about all of the things that I can tell you, in an effort to prepare you for what lies ahead, I almost do not know where to start. So I will capture it in this one simple phrase "Love yourself and see yourself the way God sees you!" Within these words, you will find the formula to help you overcome the challenges that you will face and to celebrate yourself during the time of rejoicing. You are going to face heartbreaks, disappointments and trials that will rock you to your very core. You will experience things that will make you question who you are in Him. However, if you seek Him early and draw close to Him, He will sweetly remind you that you are the precious gem that He has set aside for His use and nothing can change that. You will shed many tears but hold on because you will laugh more than you have cried. You will give until it hurts and no one will notice but God will reward you in ways man never could. Be proud of who you are. Every curve, every dip and every flaw is to be celebrated because your beauty resonates from within and that will shine through.

Never forget that you are a blessing to all who are fortunate to know you. Your beauty far exceeds what the eye can see. Stand tall and stand proud now! Don't let anyone take your voice! As you grow, you will find that your inner and outer beauty will be the most wonderful gifts that the Lord has graced you with. Seek God in all things, He is always standing there waiting. He wants you to seek Him first and He will guide you. He may not move the mountain, but He will give you the strength to climb or the

Know Your Worth

wisdom to go around. Love yourself the same way you will love others and do not give the responsibility of your happiness to anyone. Get to know yourself as you grow and appreciate every aspect that makes you, YOU! Your unique traits will open the door to so many blessings.

So be encouraged and know that no matter what you face, you are valuable! You are a rare and priceless jewel with so much to offer and to give. No matter what you have endured, it will never define you or stop God from using you! God calls you Beautiful, because you were fearfully and wonderfully made in His Image and in His Likeness! Lastly, don't worry about the loves that were lost. Those were just stepping stones that will lead you to the one who sees you for you, and loves your past, present and future. God will lead you to the one that speaks to the very essence of your being, and to the one whom your soul loves. So enjoy the journey. The best is yet to come!

All My Love,
Romona

Connect with Author Romona Jackson

Website: www.redefiningme.net
Email: totallifeproductions@gmail.com
Instagram: rzetablu4
Facebook: Romona Jackson/ ReDefining Me, LLC/ Total Life Productions, LLC
LinkedIn: www.linkedin.com/in/romona-m-jackson-9a6a57b7
Twitter: Romona Jackson

www.ingramcontent.com/pod-product-compliance
Lightning Source LLC
Chambersburg PA
CBHW060343080526
44584CB00013B/895